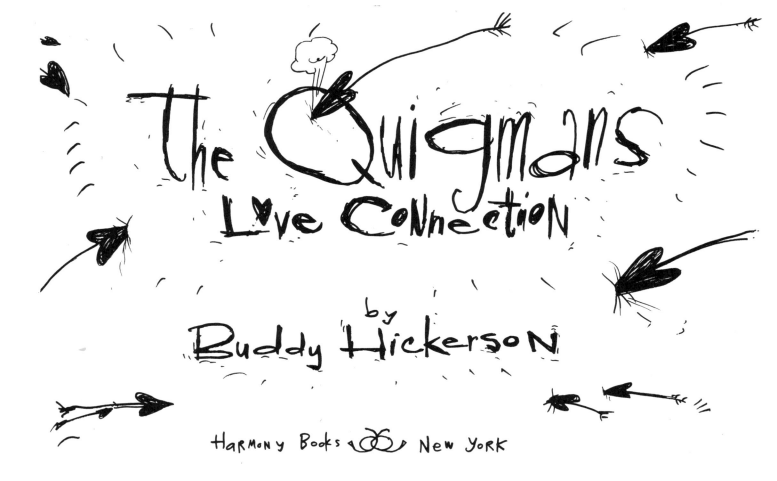

The Quigmans
Love Connection

by
Buddy Hickerson

Harmony Books ⚭ New York

Published by Harmony Books, 201 East 50th St., New York, N.Y. 10022 Member of the Crown Publishing Group. Manufactured in the United States of America.

HARMONY and colophon are trademarks of Crown Publishers, Inc.

First Edition

91-43219 CIP

Library of Congress Cataloging-in-Publication Data

Hickerson, Buddy
The Quigmans: Love Connection / by Buddy Hickerson — 1st ed.
p. cm.
1. American wit and humor, Pictorial I. Title
PN 6162 . H47 1992
741. 5′ 973 — dc 20

ISBN 0-517-58873-0
10 9 8 7 6 5 4 3 2 1

If you hanker to probe the dank recesses of Quigman lore or attain an exotic catalog of rare, ancillary Quigman paraphenalia.

Send a stamped, self addressed envelope to:

Quiglana
P.O. Box 28003
Dallas, TX
75228

A hearty special thanks to Stanfill, my disproportionately apoplectic co-writer with a thousand uses, without whose help the Quigmans would be largely unaffected.

Also large thanks to:

Shirley Snyder, who assisted in the formulation of six years of relationship material. Jerry Lentz, whose intricate knowledge of the deviant sexual underworld has provided many a late-night laugh.

Joey Waldon, who let me sleep in his bathroom.

My Brother Sander, who has been like a brother to me.

My Entire Family, which has always treated me like one of its own.

"Hold still, it's my first day!"

Luckily, Francine had treated her clothing with
Pam, so Bob slid right off.

"Deforestating paper or landfill-burdening
plastic?"

"Darn! That reminds me. I forgot to pick up some mushrooms."

Only 35 and already Bob was experiencing chest pains.

Condensed Milk Cow.

"I've decided to remove all the fat from my diet . . . so hit the road, Bob."

The 102nd Dalmation: The one they kept hidden.

"Mornin', Phil. The unusual?"

WHEN BOB WAS YOUNG, HE told EVERYONE HE WAS going to grow up to BE a CARTOON aND THEY all LaughEd at him. But no one is Laughing Now.

Excessively Private Detective

"What do I care about YOUR problems? I've got my own life, which, incidentally, is none of your business, so get out of my office."

Revenge of the Puppy.

"Quigman, you've been an employee of mine for some time. I'd like to bounce something off you."

"WOO! Check out the third and seventh
segments on THAT babe. YEAH!"

"Hey! Relax, guys! It's street legal!"

Everyone dreaded a slide show at
Bob's house.

New Kids Receive the Block.

"The mosquitoes are merciless today."

"How's that new cat of yours working out,
Frank?"

"Now that I'm governor, I will dedicate my
term to truth . . . I'll start by admitting my
entire campaign was a pack of lies."

"Hey, Barn . . . have you ever really looked at your hands?"

Before it was perfected by danceologists at the Dancing Institute of Technology, it used to take seven to tango.

Since Bob was an arsonist AND a pacifist, he would stand around for weeks praying for spontaneous combustion.

Years of tuna-purchasing guilt have taken
their toll on Todd.

Jowles' body was a temple, but his mouth
was an atheist.

Blue Star Ointment Cult.

Murphy's Law (of Love Handles).

Playing army, 1991.

Bob Quigman: The Fodder of
Our Country.

"Hey! What do you want from me? I'm only subhuman!"

"Old habits die hard, eh, Bob?"

"Looks like the work of that vampire from the Nursing Home."

Shortly after having her legs waxed, Francine experiences the heartbreak of waxy yellow build-up.

In Bob's line of work, ignorance was
considered job security.

Siegfried loses his grip on realty.

"Hey, Mr. Wilson . . . Let's go hunt some spotted asparagus beetles. Yummy!"

Bob persevered but never quite attained
sleeping like a baby.

"Not only does it have 97% less fat, but it's
great for scouring off baked-on grime and has
the pine-fresh scent of the deep, north woods."

After six months of dating, Francine finally
allowed Bob to kiss her lip gloss.

"You are a bonafide psycho, Deidre. But
you're lucky! That's my type."

"Come to think of it . . . that napkin's mine, too!"

"My appetite is in full retreat."

"I'm gonna need after-dinner armamints."

Obscure super heroes.

"Hey, waiter! There aren't enough flies in my soup."

Combo businesses that failed.

"You're FREE!"

"You're a horrible kisser, Stan. Are you aware
your lips never move?"

"Oh, Marcie! Isn't it divine? I'm getting divorced in the same dress my mother was divorced in!"

"It's a gift to celebrate your election as
President of our Ecology Club. We call it an
ozone layer cake."

"It says: 'You may already BE
a winner.'"

"Well . . . this is the last leg of our journey, guys. Make it last."

"I don't care if you HAVE taken a vow of silence . . . I'm your mother. You should have called!"

"Let us pray. Just kidding!"

Saudi Arabian golf tour.

"Oh, Sylvia! That blue-haired dowager is to DIE for!!"

"O.K., Abdul! Make a wish and blow up the cake!"

"One of these days, Alice . . . bang, zip, ZOOM . . . to the Earth!"

Isaac Newton discovers comedy.

If Glasnost fails.

"Go ahead, Mary Lou! Try a little of this steak.
It can't hurt you! AAHAHAHAHA!!"

"Lemme see . . . I'll take a pound of sirloin, a
couple of pounds of T-bone and . . . Oh!
Lemme have some of that tripe."

Jowles learns to roll over.

"Very kind of you, Bob . . . but that's the volume control."

"Why . . . Miss Johnson! Without your
glasses . . . you're beautiful!"

People were always telling
FRANZ he had ROOM for im-
provement... so he decided
to build on a sun porch.

"Well, I felt the House of Rearview Mirrors was a rip-off, but the wife was startled by the Glove Compartment of Lost Souls."

"FREEZE, Quigman!! Wearing bad plaid again? Bourgeois SCUM!! You have the right to an accessory, but only if it accents cheerfully."

A scene mankind will never see.

"Lemme guess . . . Instead of being raised as a child, you were lowered."

"Well, no WONDER, Bob. You have the aerobics tape in upside down!"

"I'm afraid your husband was frozen solid at the TV dinner factory, ma'am. Roll back the foil, Henderson."

"I get coffee for the boss, I wear tiny outfits, I file my nails . . . I'm tellin' you, Helen . . . it's a thinkless job."

"Doc! What did you pay for that gown?
I can get you TWICE the
quality wholesale!"

If Hugh Hefner had been fond of wart hogs.

"Yo! I'm itchin' for an adventure, Boys! Let's go on a pay strike!"

"Oh no! You guys took that mind-numbing
Chip 'n' Dale Carnegie course, didn't you?"

"Hey, DAD! WAKE UP! Santa came! He left
me a spinning top and some figgy
pudding . . . but the stereo's gone."

"I know I'm not Mr. Right . . . but how about
Mr. Right Now?"

"Hold it right there, young gingerbread lady! Is
that a hickey I see
on your neck?"

"I LIVE for 'Pin the Blame on
the Boyfriend.' "

"Francine, I've got good news and bad news.
The hair transplant was a success, but I think
I've gone blind."

The name is Bum. James Bum.

"I better hang up, Betty. It appears my
boss, Mr. Sensitive, is trying to
tell me something."

"Every year it's the same thing, Doc. I wanna go to the mountains and she wants to go to the beach."

It was absurd, but the painting's eyes seemed to follow Bob across the room.

In a blind attempt to outdo the frosted hairdos of her evil cousins, Kimberly had her tips freeze-dried.

Whistler's surrogate mother.

"You wasted your money on this stripper,
Fred. Don't you remember? We're DOGS!"

Thanksgiving around the world.

As children, Frank and Bob were left in the woods to be raised by wolves. Bob, however, was raised by slime molds.

"Wooo! That's what I call beefcake!"

Godzilla at home.

"You . . . uh . . . wouldn't happen to have an extension cord around here, huh? Boy, this is embarrassing."

"Just another outgrowth of our wretched
economy, son . . . the migrant farm."

"Francine! I love those slingback shoes."

Rhomboid IV!

Sylvester Stallone plays a parallelogram with oblique angles gone BERSERK !!

"My mother used to say, 'Francine, you're not that pretty, but men will adore your limitless public transit abilities.'"

"Run for your lives! It's Big Man on Campus!!
AAH!"

Frank was stricken with the apprehension that
the formal dinner guests would discover
his head was a clip-on.

"Yeah! I'm made out of Play-Doh! You wanna
make somethin' out of it?"

"Eat all your stew, son. Y'know, there are
lots of little doggies in China that
ARE stew."

"There they go, boys! O.K. . . . Let's round
'em off at the pass!"

"I've noticed something about these
dressmaker murders, Henderson . . . there's
always a pattern."

Tip monger.

After work Bob would retreat to a local pub to unwind.

"Bob has the most amazing photographic memory. You wouldn't believe—Ooh! Here they come!"

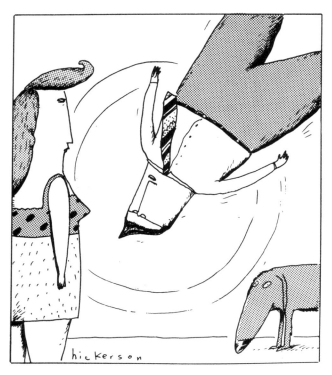

While attempting to roll his eyes, a
malfunction occurs, and Bob's eyes
roll HIM.

"I'm leaving the circus, Mom and Dad. I'm
running away with a C.P.A. firm."

"Looks like the Buffalo Gal has come out tonight."

Mixing business with pleasure.

A highly emotional woman, Francine burst into tears.

"I don't mean to ridicule your complexion, sir, but could we photograph your face for the menu?"

"That hair really is you, Bob."

"In local news, a local newscaster was robbed on the air today. Film . . . almost immediately."

Moe plugs the meter.

"I hate this job. The retirement plan really bites."

Dan Piraro, inventor of the pocket fisherman.

"Look here, Inspector . . . another one!
Offhand I'd say he took a seltzer bottle
point-blank."

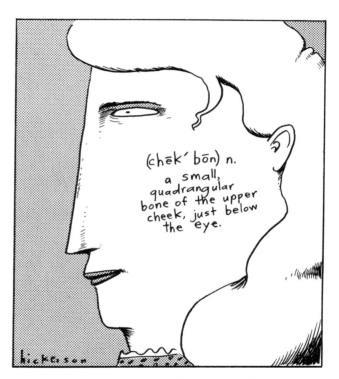

Francine had well-defined cheekbones.

For maximum results, Bob wore corrective shoes all over his body.

Bob was the Scud missile of
human beings.

"What are you, Fernando? A man
or a mousse?"

"You fool!! You are holding your wine too tight! Let it breathe!!"

In his eagerness to lick the beaters, Bob forgets they're still attached to a mixer.

The "Brady Bunch bill" was introduced in Congress today. The bill will prevent former child stars from purchasing hand guns for 7 days.

"Welcome to extremely high impact aerobics. Ready, people? One, two, three . . . LEAP!"

Many of Bob's problems can be traced back to his childhood insecurity blanket.

"She won't go, Captain."

"I'm sorry it's not working out, Marsha. I guess I've got some growing up to do."

"It's our son, Doctor. He's lost the will to leave."

"No, ladies, I'm sorry. This isn't a movie
theater. It's a nightclub."

As night grew ever deeper, Bob began
to fear he wouldn't fall into the
wrong hands.

"Some say I'm an overly protective mother,
but I say, Hey! You can't be too careful,
so I had Billy and the twins laminated."

"I remember when we were beautiful earth
children . . . before the erosion."

The Quigmans visit Lyin' Country Safari.

AFTeR learning THaT NaTives DRaNK the blood oF theiR enemies to suRpass THem iN sTRENGTH, Bob GuzzLeS his GiRLfrieNd's NaiL PoLiSH.

hickerson

"I wish they'd hurry up and discover gravity."

Late-Night Middle Ages Commercial.

"Just do what he says and give him your wallet, George. He looks like a desperate lending institution."

"Well, we've saved the whales, the elephants, and the whooping cranes . . . what endangered species is next?"

Eventually, the Quigmans began to grow suspicious that the restaurant was closing.